MW01004288

HOW GOD SEES YOUR STRUGGLES
Find Your Strength. Live Happier &
Know You Are Worth It.

By Lynn R. Davis

Find out when my books are free. Submit your email address at IMotivateMyself.com Consider hearing the audiobook for this title? CLICK NOW to see how you may be able to listen for free.

Contents

INTRODUCTION

I get stressed. I feel like the walls are closing in. I cry. I get overwhelmed. I write Christian inspiration, but I'm just like everyone else. I don't have all the answers, but what I do have is God-and my God has ALL the answers.

That's why I'm excited about this book and its inspirational insight. I'm bubbling with excitement about what God wants you to know. Because I know that these things will change your life the way that they have mine.

This is a feel-good book. I like to write these types of books because we all can benefit from encouragement. It's just good to feel good about something.

You're going to enjoy this. It's filled with encouraging words of wisdom and golden nuggets of inspiration. I truly appreciate you, the reader.

God has blessed me with your presence. And I truly value your time and support.

This work is filled with Good News. It will motivate you to see things in a new way. The chapters are short and sweet as is the book. If that sounds like your kind of reading, dive in. Inspiration and encouragement await you.

He wants you to know without a doubt that He is real. You can't physically see Him but He is always there. Like the wind, we can't see it, but we know it's there. Whether cool, gentle, breezes swirl through the leaves or hurricane-force winds lift buildings foundations.
The wind makes its presence known. Likewise, we may not see God, but we do see the evidence.

Sometimes the subtle feeling of peace in a life storm but at other times undeniable through miraculous survivals, healings, and restorations.

When you know certain things about God, I mean know them, your life changes. You experience a shift. The things that used to knock you down won't. Here are some of the wonderful truths we should hold fast:

- He does love you and He appreciates you.
- It's never what it seems.
- He's always with you.
- Your labor is never in vain.
- He's always making away.
- He hears and answers prayer.
- You don't have to be perfect.
- Soul food is the best food.
- He can use anybody.

God has so much more in store for you than you have allowed yourself to receive. The blessings He wants for you are eternal.

Those eternal treasures will then lead to the earthly manifestations you desire. "Fear not, little flock; for it is your Father's good pleasure to give you the kingdom." (Luke 12:32)

Your current place in life doesn't have to be a permanent stop unless you want it to be. He is always working things out in your favor.

The path you're on that seems rocky is still a path leading somewhere. You're headed somewhere. Don't stop now.

Think of where you are as a rest stop. You don't stay there. You pass through. One day you will look back and realize that this place in time helped you to become who you always desired to be.

You will be stronger, wiser, and closer to the Father.

CHAPTER 1

OTHER PEOPLE'S FOOLISHNESS
"There are some people who always seem
angry and continuously look for conflict;
walk away. The battle they are fighting isn't
with you. It is with themselves." –Unknown

Other people. Why do we get ourselves so
worked up about what *other people* say,
think, feel, or believe? If you are to have any
peace whatsoever, you've got to overcome
the need to please *other people.*

The only acceptance you truly cannot live
without is God's. It's not anyone else's job
to judge you or decide whether or not you
deserve God's blessings. Unfortunately, that
is exactly what some will do.

You are to pray for them, but love them
from a distance. Do not allow them to
pollute your faith.
Proverbs 18:2 describes such people:

"Fools find no pleasure in understanding but delight in airing their own opinions." Fools are not interested in wisdom, only hearing themselves talk. Stop wasting your precious time and tears on fools.

I know people who have lost sleep and even fallen into depression because they stressed and worried themselves into madness about a conflict they had with a fool. They just couldn't understand why that person wouldn't listen to reason or even try to resolve the issue.

Read Proverbs 29:9, "When a wise man has a controversy with a foolish man, the foolish man either rages or laughs, and there is no rest." (NASB)

God wants you to know that He did not create you to be mocked, used, abused, or mistreated. And if you are being targeted for doing what is right, be encouraged: "God blesses those who are persecuted for doing right, for the Kingdom of Heaven is theirs." (Matthew 5:10)

Proverbs 6:14 talks about troublemakers who continually keep up conflict. "Their perverted hearts plot
evil and they constantly stir up trouble."

You cannot get sucked in by foolishness and maintain your health, peace, and sanity. Remember God is not the author of confusion. Walk away from it.

You don't have to worry about getting back at those who attack you. As long as you keep your heart right with God and your actions are in love Proverbs 10:29 says, "The way of the LORD *is* the strength to the upright: but destruction *shall be* to the workers of iniquity." Negative people bring destruction on themselves.

Spend your time in prayer and meditation, not in contemplating evil for evil. There is no time for that.
Never allow someone with a negative spirit to pull you into the pit of misery with them. Speak in love. Let it go. Walk away and pray. Let God do the rest.

CHAPTER- 2

HE LOVES, APPRECIATES, AND
ADORES YOU.

God wants you to know that His love for
you is steadfast (Psalm 103:17). *Committed,
devoted, dedicated, solid, dependable-* all of
these words are synonymous with God's
love toward you.

No matter what judgmental others around
you have told you, He loved you when you
were conceived; the day you were born; and
right this very moment.

With all of your perfect flaws, you are His
child made in His image. You have to see
yourself (and every circumstance in your
life) the way God does. See your life
through the eyes of God.

He is steady and unwavering. Loving you
just as much today and before you were
born. Even then He loved you so much that

He began making plans for you to have a fantastic life (Jeremiah 29:11).

Nothing can separate you from His love. That love is pure and unconditional. From God's perspective, you deserve the very best in every area of your life.

And to that end, He will work everything out-everything. What happens may not be good, but He loves you so much that when it's all said and done, you will be better and stronger. What you're going through will strengthen you.

While you were in your mother's womb, He began putting things in place to help you succeed, achieve and overcome every obstacle that He knew might cross your path.

He was and is mindful of you always (Psalm 8:4). Flowing love toward you in every second of the day even as you sleep. It has always been that way and always will. You can't change that. You may as well surrender to His love, *"resistance is futile."*

To get a beautiful illustration of what love is, consider reading 1 Corinthians 13:4-6:

"**4** Love is patient, love is kind. It does not envy, it does not boast, it is not proud. **5** It does not dishonor others, it is not self-seeking, it is not easily angered, it keeps no record of wrongs. **6** Love does not delight in evil but rejoices with the truth. **7** It always protects, always trusts, always hope, always perseveres."

Scripture tells us "God is love." So each of those descriptions in the verse above would apply to the character of our God. And what I get from 1 Corinthians 13:4-6, is that my God is:

- kind
- not easily angered
- not keeping a record of wrongs
- truthful
- always protecting
- always trustworthy
- always hopeful
- always persevering

To love and be loved is an incredibly wonderful experience. There is something truly exhilarating about being the object of another's love and devotion. It's a feeling of elation, desire, appreciation, and even inspiration. God wants you to feel that all the time, not just when you "feel worthy" of His love.

His love is a gift. You don't earn it; find it; nor can you lose it.

"For the mountains may depart and the hills are removed, but my steadfast love shall not depart from you, and my covenant of peace shall not be removed," says the Lord, who has compassion on you." (Isaiah 54:10)

Not many have experienced such love. Mainly because they are seeking it from other human beings. And because friends, family, and lovers tend to express conditional love, we think that God is doing the same. But God's love is much more than diamonds, pearls, and physical satisfaction.

Ephesians 3:19 says, "And to know the love of Christ that surpasses knowledge, that you may be filled with all the fullness of God."

There is a love that transcends our common knowledge. That our human brains cannot fully comprehend. That love is the infinite, infallible, agape love of God. "But the steadfast love of the Lord is from everlasting to everlasting on those who fear him, and his righteousness to children's children," (Psalm 103:17)

Can you understand a love that would inspire God to send His son to die for our sins? I cannot. And to be brutally honest I cannot imagine sacrificing either of my sons for *any* reason.

The ultimate love is available for you in every situation. Allow the feeling of that love to envelop you now. As you sit reading, imagine the loving grace and mercy of God coming on you. Know that His steadfast, undying love is yours in every experience.

Can you feel the peace that comes with knowing God will be there for you no matter what you do? No matter who leaves you or what comes against you. You are loved by an all-powerful; all-knowing creator.

"For I am sure that neither death nor life, nor angels nor rulers, nor things present nor things to come, nor powers, nor height nor depth, nor anything else in all creation, will be able to separate us from the love of God in Christ Jesus our Lord." (Romans 8:39)

CHAPTER -3

IT SEEMS BAD BUT GOD SEES IT
DIFFERENTLY.

God wants you to know that you are always
on the brink of a breakthrough moment. At
any given time, your circumstance can
improve in a way that will make your
spectators drop their bottom jaw and scratch
their heads. Believe that.

God wants you to know that He cares about
what is happening in your life. He has your
back. You are not alone. He is always with
you. Even when you feel your worst, know
that He is right there offering comfort and
guiding you toward peace. Because He
knows that in the end, you will be
victorious. "But they that wait upon the
LORD shall renew their strength; they shall
mount up with wings as eagles; they shall
run, and not be weary, and they shall walk,
and not faint." (Isaiah 40:31)

The moment you open your heart to Him
you will begin to feel the subtle soothing of
His love for you. The love that moves
mountains; heals the sick; and raises the
dead. The more you allow the more it will
heal and restore. It is that love that will bring
you through, but what if you could take a
more proactive approach to face life's
challenges.

Try to see it God's way. He does not see
misery, He sees an opportunity for ministry.
What if you view your problems as
possibilities? And then reminded yourself,
with God the possibilities are endless.

God wants you to be hopeful at all times,
even in challenging circumstances. I
understand some situations are worse than
others. Abusive relationships are one
example. If you are in a situation where you
are being abused- leave.

That is not God's best for you. Seek help
and find a way to get yourself to safety. Pray
for that person from afar. Let God work in
them while you heal in a safe environment.

Stressed out, angry, afraid, and doubtful, is not how God intends you to live. Try to see it His way, *what it will not stop what will be.*

Every dilemma has an expiration date. That's right. *It's only temporary.* I know you've heard that before, but when is it going to sink in? How many times must God deliver us before we begin to trust Him more than we doubt?

"So we fix our eyes not on what is seen, but on what is unseen, since what is seen is temporary, but what is unseen is eternal." (2 Corinthians 4:18)
It struck me one day that God has always come through for me. Without fail, He has always made a way. Even in the situations that ended differently than I desired (at the time).

Sometimes the breakthrough took longer to manifest than others, but always deliverance came in some form-relief, peace, finances, healing, inspiration, salvation…always.
There is a cycle that we go through. First, the problem comes. Then we stress lament, worry, and fear. After we struggle a little

and doubt a lot, we throw up our hands and give it over to God. By this time we're tired, weary, and indifferent. Victory manifests and we look back and wonder how God did it. We praise him and testify of His goodness.

Isn't it nice to know that you don't have to go through all of that emotional turmoil? All you have to do is accept from the beginning that God is going to work it all out.

That what's happening is never what it seems.
If it seems like it's going to destroy you, it's not. If someone walked out on you, it's not the end of the world. They're freeing space for someone better.

Or this situation is going to help both of you become better, clearer, more resolved. It's a challenge yes, but don't see it as your undoing but rather a chance for renewing-your mind, your desires, your outlook.

But how long will the challenge last. When will it end? God says, "This will pass soon." As soon as you give it all to Him. That is when the torment ends. Because when you give it to Him-truly let it go; the stress and worry leave.

You stop posting about it on Facebook. You stop bringing it up in conversations with your friends. Why? Because -God has it. And it is no longer your business. "Cast all your anxiety on him because he cares for you." (1 Peter 5:7)

The darkness of your problems cannot remain once they are placed in the presence of God's light. "This is the message we have heard from him and declare to you: God is light; in him, there is no darkness at all." (1 John 1:5)
When life becomes a tangled mess, it's easy to focus on the mess and forget the good.

I watched my youngest as he played with a bunch of frilly green party streamers. He squealed and laughed as the wind blew and swirled the paper strips around his head. It wasn't long though before his feet were tangled.

He stumbled and plopped to the ground. I ran to him to help, Disappointed, he began to sob as I unraveled the green strips from his ankles. The fun had ended.

Don't let the tangled mess keep you from enjoying life. God is watching you and He sees what's happening. He will help you untangle the mess if you let Him.
Find a way to be hopeful and faithful-even before trouble comes.

That way when life gets messy, you can still smile and laugh because you know that God is going to straighten everything out.

~

Happy moments, praise God. Difficult moments,
Seek God. Quiet moments, Worship God.
Painful moments, Trust God.
Every Moment, Thank God. Count your Blessings.
-Unknown

~

CHAPTER- 4

YOUR LABOR IS NOT IN VAIN.
Every good thing you contribute is bringing
you closer to the manifestation of your
desire. You feel like you've been spinning
your wheels. You can't seem to get traction.

Nothing is happening the way you thought it
would and it's taking way longer than it
should. Says who? God has not forsaken
you. He will never do that.

David said in Psalm 37:25, "I was young
and now I am old, yet I have never seen the
righteous forsaken or their children begging
bread." Whether it is your family, career, a
dream, or an opportunity disguised as a
problem, your labor is not in vain.
"Therefore, my dear brothers and sisters,
stand firm. Let nothing move you. Always
give yourselves fully to the work of the
Lord, because you know that your labor in

the Lord is not in vain." (1 Corinthians
15:58)

He has not left you for dead. Your enemies
may circle like vultures now, but they will
be astonished when God has completed the
work in you that He started. Sure maybe the
direction has changed or the launch date has
been postponed, but that is alright. I read
once that a dream deferred is not a dream
denied.
Joseph's dream did not manifest overnight, it
took years. He didn't know that He was
going to be imprisoned. God doesn't always
show us everything. And for good reason. If
we could see the difficult seasons ahead, we
may try to circumvent them.

Years ago God showed me in a dream that I
would become a published author. I was
very excited. In the dream, I was holding a
book and I was on the phone excitedly
talking about it to someone. When I woke
up I couldn't remember the title. I still don't.
But I held on to that dream as confirmation
that my dream mattered to God and He was
going to show me how to accomplish it.

Had I known, on the way to manifesting this dream, that I would almost lose my home; endure family and financial struggles; I may have trashed that dream altogether. I might still be stressed working a 9-5 job for fear of going through that rough patch. God saw me through. All is well and on December 15, 2015, my first traditionally published book will be in bookstores. My dream may have been delayed but it was not denied.

I endured all of those obstacles but, my labor was not in vain. I endured and remained steadfast in God's faithfulness. Today I am living the reality of my dream. Free of stress and the ability to manifest the life I've always dreamed of as a bestselling author. The sky is the limit and I'm grateful for every moment and opportunity that God has granted me.

God is not playing favorites. He is not blessing others and withholding them from you. Just as Jesus said to the blind men, according to your faith.

"When He entered the house, the blind men came up to Him, and Jesus said to them, 'Do you believe that I can do this?' They said to

Him, 'Yes, Lord.' Then He touched their eyes, saying, 'It shall be done to you according to your faith.'" (Matthew 9:28-29)

Do you believe it without a doubt? Whatever you are facing, is just pit-stop on the way to your destination. You don't have to stay where you are unless you decide to pitch a tent and throw a permanent pity party. Wait on the Lord; stay in faith and get ready to mount up on wings.

God doesn't want you to settle, He wants you to soar. You're not just spinning your wheels. Certainly, if you are working toward a goal that glorifies God. And when a believer achieves success God is glorified.

"But they that wait upon the LORD shall renew their strength; they shall mount up with wings as eagles; they shall run, and not be weary, and they shall walk, and not faint." (Isaiah 40:39)

You may start small but you will fulfill your desire in God's timing. "[10] Do not despise these small beginnings, for the LORD rejoices to see the work begin, to see the

plumb line in Zerubbabel's hand."
(Zechariah 4:10)

~

God said don't look around
Because you'll be impressed. Don't
look down
You will be depressed;
Just look to me and you'll be blessed.

~

CHAPTER- 5

GOD IS IN THE FURNACE WITH YOU.

Let the enemies or frenemies (friends who turn out to be enemies) turn up the heat. It's okay. Because Jesus is in your life, you will not be destroyed. The Hebrew boys are a witness, Jesus will deliver you. He's not afraid of hell-fire. He has conquered hell.

"I am the Living One; I was dead, and now look, I am alive forever and ever! And I hold the keys of death and Hades." (Revelation 1:18).

As long as He's with you, you don't have to worry or be afraid. Before it's all over your enemy will be bowing to your God.

"It is written: ' As surely as I live,' says the Lord, 'every knee will bow before me; every tongue will acknowledge God.'" (Romans 14:11)

Let God work. Watch Him prepare a table in the presence of your enemy (Psalm 23:5). People who know you will have no choice but to acknowledge God's presence in your circumstances. Be encouraged by what God said to Cyrus in Isaiah 45:2-3:

"(2) I will go before you and make the rough places smooth; I will shatter the doors of bronze and cut through their iron bars. (3)"I will give you the treasures of darkness And hidden wealth of secret places, So that you may know that it is I, The LORD, the God of Israel, who calls you by your name…"

God knows who you are and He knows what you desire. If He has chosen you and anointed you to do it, He will see you through it. And He will bless you beyond your imagination.

He also knows the best way to get you to your destination. Sometimes that route, through no fault of your own, is less than ideal. How inconvenient must the Fiery Furnace have been? Surely there was another way to show faithfulness rather than be faced with death by fire. But God is always with you.

And no matter how hot it gets or how crooked that path seems, He can deliver. I used to get so down when obstacles would come. It was all I could do to keep a fake smile on my face in public. On the inside, I was crying, but I put up a front because I didn't want people to know that I felt hopeless and afraid. Anything could come along and knock me into a negative slump.

Now I stop; take a deep breath; and tell myself, "God has never forsaken you and He's not about to start now. Try to see it His way."
No matter how complicated your situation has become he can straighten out any mess. Trust Him. Give it to Him. Take your hands off of it. Don't be led by your emotions or what you see happening around you. Only allow yourself to be led by the Spirit.

~

Blessings come soon, some come late
And some don't come until heaven.
But for those who embrace
The gospel of Jesus Christ comes.
-Jeffrey Holland

~

CHAPTER- 6

TRUE WEALTH IS ETERNAL.

The peace and happiness you seek are
available to you now, whether you have the
finances you desire or not. Oh yes, He wants
you to have prosperity, but you must know
His definition includes more than diamonds,
cars, and houses.

True prosperity is having every need met
and living in joy and peace with God as the
head of your life. If that is true in your life,
you are wealthier than you realize.

Seek God first. Let Him show you what true
prosperity is. Feel the joy of the Lord every
day. Let it be your strength in times of
trouble. That joy is lasting because God is
everlasting. The happiness you seek from
possessions is fleeting. Have you ever

wanted something badly, and then after you got it, you lost your enthusiasm? That was conditional happiness.

Your happiness depended on a thing. Things don't make us truly joyful. They temporarily give us a sense of achievement or status. But when the feeling goes away because the possession is gone or we lose interest, we're left feeling empty again.
Many of us witness this on Christmas morning. Our children open their gifts. They're excited for all of ten minutes and the next thing you know they've thrown the toy to the side and something else grabs their attention. Sadly some adults do the same.

God enjoys His children having "things" that make them smile. Just as we enjoy giving to our children and loved ones. "…Let the Lord be magnified; which hath pleasure in the prosperity of His servant." (Psalm 35:27)

But there is so much more that He wants you to have.
I purchased my second car brand new. It smelled good and looked good. I looked good in it.

The feelings of exhilaration over my new ride lasted for a few months and then it was gone. Soon my focus turned from its newness, bells, and whistles to the maintenance and the monthly car payment. The thrill was gone- if you will. You don't have to have a new car in your garage to have joy.

Try to see it God's way, *Possessions are beautiful and can be a lot of fun to have, but joy is priceless and unconditional. That is the goal-internal joy in the everlasting.* If you can be joyful regardless of what you possess, then you possess true wealth that can never be taken away.

True prosperity is priceless. You can't buy a sound mind or a peaceful night's rest. Nor can you purchase happy, well-adjusted children. But those are things we should treasure far more than any earthly possession. Those priceless blessings come from being in a relationship with a loving God.

Receiving the love of God puts you in a place of being able to receive from God. The blessings you seek must be received by faith.

When you receive His love, you believe that you are worthy to receive. Believing opens your heart for receiving. More joy and peace will come from just feeling loved and worthy than you can imagine. Those gifts are eternal.

Things don't bring us eternal happiness. Only the loving acceptance of God gives us lasting unconditional love, joy, and peace. Always seek that happiness first. Be happy in the knowledge of Jesus Christ.

~

When you begin to worry, go find
something to do.
Get busy being a blessing to someone;
do something fruitful.
Talking about your problem or sitting
alone,
Thinking about it does no good; it
serves only to make you miserable.
Above all else, remember that
worrying is useless.
Worrying will not solve your
problem. –Joyce Meyer

~

CHAPTER- 7

GOD IS ALWAYS MAKING A WAY.

When you don't have enough and you don't know where to get more; He'll make a way out of no way. You don't have to know how, when, where, or why. Just know that God is always making a way.

Don't despise the little that you have. Be grateful for it. Your grateful heart is a catalyst to increase. It's a key to the door of more. Because God is always adding more to your less. He's always making a way.

Two fish and five barley loaves stretched to feed five thousand people. God made a way. Don't doubt what God can do with your little bit. In God's hands, it becomes more than you could ever have imagined. Trust Him.

"Taking the five loaves and the two fish and looking up to heaven, he gave thanks and broke the loaves. Then he gave them to his disciples to distribute to the people. He also divided the two fish among them all." Mark 6:41 (NIV)

God already knows what He is going to do. And He's going to do it with what you have. You don't think that you have enough to work with. I've heard it said, "Little becomes much in the Master's hands". How odd must it have seemed to even consider two fish and five loaves of bread being enough to feed a crowd of five thousand hungry folks? I wouldn't have been so faithful in that situation, not even preparing dinner for my small family. It just doesn't seem realistic to me. And not for a huge crowd.

What do you have that doesn't seem like enough? Do you doubt that God can make things work in your favor or are you staying in faith that He is faithful to prepare a table before you in the presence of your enemies? (Psalm 23:5)

Lift what you have to the heavens and give thanks for it. Place it before God and allow Him to open doors of opportunity and bring the increase. No matter what it looks like to you, know that He can take something meager and make it magnificent.

"But God chose the foolish things of the world to shame the wise; God chose the weak things of the world to shame the strong." (1 Corinthians 1:27) God specializes in impossibilities.

He will take what seems small and insignificant to you; shine His glory on it and baffle everyone around you-including the so-called professionals and experts. Then He will not only exalt you, but He will also capture the attention of unbelievers. Your "small thing" will usher in a big blessing that causes others to praise God. Possibly even lead someone to Christ.

He wants to transform your mind and put you in a place of receiving. If your focus is on the shortage, you're in a place of lack. Anxiety about what is happening only increases fear and doubt. Don't smother your faith.

Change your mind. Think as God thinks. Try to see it His way. Things are working out for your good (Romans 8:28). Be grateful. Recognize the abundance all around you. Watch God bring the increase.

"Be anxious for nothing, but in everything by prayer and supplication, with thanksgiving, let your requests be made known to God; [7] and the peace of God, which surpasses all understanding, will guard your hearts and minds through Christ Jesus." (Philippians 4:6-7)

~

A contented mind is the greatest
blessing
A man can enjoy in this world.
– Joseph Addison

~

CHAPTER- 8

YOU'RE JUST ONE MUSTARD SEED
AWAY.

It only takes a little bit of faith to turn things
around. Make the transition from frustration
to appreciation. Realize that this is
temporary. Give yourself a break if you've
been feeling down. Doubt is part of our
earthly experience. Doubt may visit but
don't ever allow it to stay. Life throws some
pretty heavy blows. And if we allow them
to, letdowns, disappointments, and loss will
train us to expect the worse.

He replied, "Because you have so little faith.
Truly I tell you, if you have faith as small as
a mustard seed, you can say to this
mountain, 'Move from here to there,' and it
will move. Nothing will be impossible for
you." Matthew 17:20 NIV

God wants you to understand something. You are supposed to succeed. You were created to prosper. So the lack that you are experiencing is not normal. It is not the plan of God. No matter how many times you've been told or by whom.

I remember as a teen hearing a preacher say, "Debt is normal. You will always be in debt." At the time, I had no reason to question what he said. *After all, why would he intentionally mislead us?*

Though I didn't question it then something about the statement never sat well with me. I know now without a doubt that Jesus paid it all on the cross. I don't have to live in debt. I have the right to prosperity. I don't have to spend my entire life owing anyone anything but to love them.

Owe no man anything, but to love one another, for he that loveth another hath fulfilled the law. (Romans 13:8-10)

If debt freedom is what you desire, you can have it. God supports you. By faith, you can and you will obtain financial freedom. "And the Lord said, If ye had faith as a grain of mustard seed, ye might say unto this sycamore tree, Be thou plucked up by the root, and be thou planted in the sea; and it should obey you." (Matthew 17:20)

If something feels off about what you're hearing or experiencing, take the time to study for yourself. "(15) Study to shew thyself approved unto God, a workman that needeth not to be ashamed, rightly dividing the word of truth." 2 Timothy 2:15

Don't allow someone else's interpretation to keep you in bondage. The goal God has placed on your heart will be validated by Him. Believe it before you see it. Trust Him to provide you with the wisdom and creativity to lead you to the right people and places. Resolve in your heart that God is faithful and He will bring His promise to pass in your life.

"Jesus saith unto him, Thomas, because thou hast seen me, thou hast believed: blessed *are* they that have not seen, and *yet* have believed." (John 20:29)

~
God will not permit any troubles to
come upon us,
Unless He has a specific plan by
which
A great blessing can come out of the
difficulty.
-Peter Marshall
~

CHAPTER- 9

YOUR DOMINANT THOUGHTS WILL
MANIFEST.

"As a man thinks in his heart so is he."
(Proverbs 23:7) Where you focus is key to
your success. *"I've set life and death before
you* today: both blessings and curses.
Choose *life*, that it may be well with *you—
you* and your children." (Deuteronomy
30:19) The negative and the positive of life
are set before you. Focus on the negative
and you will give life to it. Keep your eyes
on the promise of God and you will give life
to it. Which would you rather live life to?

While it's ideal to turn away from your
problem, what happens when your problem
is right in your face and you have no choice
but to stare it down every day? Henry David
Thoreau said, "It's not what you look at that
matters, it's what you see."

I believe this to be true in cases where you have to face something unwanted. In those cases, we should use the eyes of our faith. Don't let your mind linger on what you dislike but rather what you desire God to manifest.

When my oldest was a teenager, he went through a rebellious stage. There was nothing I could do but face the situation. I had no choice. He was my son and I loved him. I wasn't going to leave nor was he. It was difficult. I cried a lot. Then God showed me that I wasn't focused on faith. I was focused on my son's faults. He reminded me that my son was not his mistake. They did not define who God created him to be. I took my physical eyes off of my son's behavior and placed my heart's eyes on God's word.

Proverbs 22:6 promised me that my son would not depart if I'd trained him upright. And I had. I'd introduced him to Christ. I'd loved him and been the best mother I knew how to be. My faith was renewed. I began to focus on my son's good qualities.

What a loving, helpful, compassionate young man he was. I poured through photo albums of his childhood and remembered the fun times. I reflected on his many accomplishments, awards and achievements. After a little while, I noticed a change not only in my son but in myself. I had more compassion and he was less rebellious. In the end, he rededicated his life to Christ. I believe that was God.

We have to believe 1 John 4:17- *As He is so are we in the earth.* There is no lack, pain, loss, or defeat in heaven. Jesus is not experiencing anything of this nature. And we must have faith to believe that we are just as Jesus is. We are whole, healthy, blessed, prosperous, compassionate, and filled with joy. *As He is so are YOU on the earth!*

~

We look forward to a time when
The power of love will replace
The love of power. Then will our
world know the blessings of peace.-
Unknown

~

CHAPTER- 10

GOD ANSWERS PRAYER.

I believe when we pray God answers.
Nothing indicates to me that He sits on our
prayer requests (indefinitely) while He
contemplates whether or not we deserve a
reply.

God knows all. He is the beginning and the
ending. Nothing has caught Him off guard.
He does not call a committee meeting to
discuss the pros and cons of giving you what
you've asked for.

"This is the confidence we have in
approaching God: that if we ask anything
according to his will, he hears us." 1 John
5:14

Every resource known to man is at His
disposal. Healing, prosperity, peace,

joy…it's all in Him. He's not transporting it in from some secret place. He is the source. It's all right at His fingertips. The only thing holding us back is us. We're not waiting on God. He's waiting on us.

The answer cannot manifest if we do not believe it.
"Therefore I tell you, whatever you ask for in prayer, believe that you have received it, and it will be yours." (Mark 11:24)

The two blind men that shouted after Jesus to heal them. They knew without a doubt that he could. They didn't care who heard them or how long they'd been blind. All they knew was there was a healer in their presence. And they received their healing.

Jesus told them, "According to your faith be it unto you." (Matthew 9:29) God is waiting for us to believe. He's waiting for us to accept what Jesus did on the cross. To believe that we have what Jesus gave us.

Where we get tripped up sometimes is in waiting for His answer. Philippians 4:6-7 says, "Do not be anxious about anything, but in every situation, by prayer and petition, with thanksgiving, present your requests to God. And the peace of God, which transcends all understanding, will guard your hearts and your minds in Christ Jesus."

Waiting on God can be frustrating. I'm willing to admit that. Many nights, in the past, I've sat wondering when God was going to answer my prayer.

Sort of like a small child on a long road trip, who asks anxiously, "Are we there yet? Are we there yet?"

I'd find myself, again and again, asking, *When God? How God? When, When When!* And not only did I want to know *when* I wanted to be clear that He should answer the way I thought He should.

The important thing to remember when you're feeling anxious about God answering your prayer is that He has heard you. In your spirit, you know that.

Your spirit is at peace. But it is your flesh that is weak and needs immediate evidence. Read Philippians 4:6-7 again. Notice scripture says we will have peace when we pray and petition with thanksgiving.

Being thankful is the key to finding peace amid your storm. Thank God for the answer and the clarity even when you don't fully comprehend.

Be grateful for whatever is causing you to pray because it is bringing you closer to God. Be thankful that this is temporary- because it will not last.

That God is with you always. Find joy in knowing the truth of 2 Corinthians 4:17, "For our light and momentary troubles are achieving for us an eternal glory that far outweighs them all."

When we pray, He hears us. He is mindful of all that we are experiencing and always working on our behalf to turn the tide in our favor.

The answer may not be what we expect. His ways are not ours. We may be in the eye of the storm, but God controls it all.

He knows what it will take to calm your storm. You prayed. He heard your prayer. It's already fixed in Jesus' name. All is well. No matter what. Trust him. "We must believe and not doubt, because the one who doubts is like a wave of the sea, blown and tossed by the wind." (James 1:6)

~

Many things are essential to arriving
at true peace of mind, and one of the
most important is faith, which
cannot be acquired without prayer.
-John Wooden

~

CHAPTER-11

PERFECTIONISM WILL HOLD YOU
BACK.

Shoot for progress. Leave perfection to God.
We all have some type of issues. None of us
are free of flaws. There is something about
each of us that benefits from the mercy of
God.

"Why do you see the speck that is in your
brother's eye, but does not notice the log that
is in your eye? Or how can you say to your
brother, 'Let me take the speck out of your
eye,' when there is the log in your eye? You
hypocrite, first take the log out of your eye,
and then you will see clearly to take the
speck out of your brother's eye." Matthew
7:3-5

When I first began my writing journey, I was a nervous mess. I didn't want to release anything that wasn't perfect.
I couldn't afford an editor and no matter how many times I reviewed the document myself, I still missed things.

Finally, I just had to let it go and press the publish button. I didn't want people to say negative things about my work. I feared negative reviews and what people would say when they found out that I was writing, *Who does she think she is?*

Well if you've read my self-published work, especially the early ones, you know I let go of those fears. I realized there is nothing I publish that cannot be corrected. I had to let it go if I was going to succeed in any way. Let go of the perfectionism.

Worry about what others think and worry about not being perfect will cripple you. God gave you the mission not them.

Don't allow people who don't know who you are in Christ to make decisions about what you can accomplish. Ignore the naysayers. It's none of your business what they think anyway.

"and to make it your ambition to lead a quiet life: You should mind your own business and work with your hands, just as we told you," (1 Thessalonians. 4:11)

"They" have no power over you, only what you allow.
This is not an excuse to be sloppy. I'm not saying that you shouldn't have a spirit of excellence. We absolutely should!

But if you're holding off on your dream or goal because EVERYTHING isn't just perfect, you're holding yourself back. As soon as I was able, I hired a freelance proofreader to help clean up those projects.

Aim to be more like Christ, not to be perfect. Accept that you have flaws and know that God accepts you just the way you are.

Yes, He will help you with every area you allow Him access to, but it's not about becoming a perfect human.

"For by grace you have been saved through faith. And this is not your own doing; it is the gift of God, not a result of works, so that no one may boast." (Ephesians 2:8-9)

Remember your aim is a progression, not perfection.

~

Every positive thing in your life
represents a single unique blessing.
Every negative thing in your life
has the opportunity to become a
double blessing.-Unknown

~

CHAPTER -12

ALLOWING OTHERS TO LIVE WILL
FREE YOU TO LIVE YOUR OWN LIFE
FULLY.

It takes a great deal of energy to keep up
with what others are doing. The minute you
decide that their life is theirs to live and not
yours to worry about, you free up the
necessary space in your mind to give full
attention to your own life goals.

"and to make it your ambition to lead a quiet
life: You should mind your own business
and work with your hands, just as we told
you," (1 Thessalonians. 4:11)

God wants to inspire us in our actions. But
sometimes we can't hear God because we're
too busy listening to other things. We're
distracted by the negative media; other

people's problems; or the negative congregation in our head. If you haven't heard the voice of God, maybe the other voices are too loud.

Have you ever tried to hear the television over a bunch of loud voices? It's difficult, isn't it? If you're like me you do one of two things. Either you grab the remote and increase the volume or your "ask" everyone to be quiet so that you can hear.

You're going to have to take measures when it comes to hearing God. Shut all of the other distractions out. Even if you have to ask some people to be quiet.

Spend more time with Him alone. Allowing His word to infiltrate your heart so that His voice is louder than the others. God is ready to talk if you are ready to listen.

But He will not yell. He will not compete with the other noise in your life. He will wait for you.

But you see, it's difficult to let go of any of those things when you're consumed by them. *What they are posting. What they are wearing. How they are spending their time. How much money they have. What lifestyle they are living in.*

That's too much information (TMI) for any person to consume about someone else. Try not to keep up with all of that.

 If you need a break from social media, take one. I have, several times. Sometimes you're scrolling through all of the posts and you can feel the weight of other people's negativity.

 Their posts about relationship drama; how much they hate their jobs; videos of fighting and killing; and breaking news of deaths and divorces. Free yourself. Take a break from it all.

Let them live their life. They don't need your approval and you don't need theirs. A roman 14:4 says, "Who are you to pass judgment on the servant of another?

It is before his own master that he stands or falls. And he will be upheld, for the Lord can make him stand."

You have no competition. And there is no one you need to keep up with except your household. Can you see how letting go of other people's lives can free you to live your own in peace?

"Wherefore seeing we also are compassed about with so great a cloud of witnesses, let us lay aside every weight and the sin which doth so easily beset *us*, and let us run with patience the race that is set before us," (Hebrews 12:1)

Try to see it His way. *You are unique and so is your journey.* Lumping yourself in with others is the fastest way to open the door for comparisons and set yourself up for failure.

When we live and let live, we show others, unconditional love. We are less likely to judge. And it's easier to see a thing the way God sees them.

He sees each of us individually and expects we each give account for ourselves. "So then each of us will give an account of himself to God." (Romans 14:12)

God wants you to know that He sees all and knows all. No one is getting away with anything. Take your time and attention back from the distractions of other people's lives. Spend that time with God.

Develop an intimate relationship. Allow Him to give you a glimpse of the wonderful plans He has for you.

~

When life seems worse, God often sends us little blessings That often go unnoticed because we are so focused on our suffering. By acknowledging blessings that bring joy into your daily life You will experience more peace and feel closer to God.
–Kimberly Dawn, Scent of Faith.com

~

CHAPTER -13

IT'S NEVER-ENDING JUST ALWAYS
BEGINNING.

Consider a change of perspective. It's not
that your relationship ended, but rather a
new relationship is on the verge of
beginning. Instead of your previous job
ended, consider that your next venture is just
beginning. Where you focus makes all of the
difference. To think only of endings is to
invite fear and worry.

Don't focus on the end. Focus on the
beginning.
Sometimes when things end, especially
relationships, we go through a low period
because we feel that we've lost something.
That's the thing about being focused on "the
end". It leaves you feeling like there is
nothing else coming next. But the truth is in

God's infinite wisdom, He knew that you'd be where you are right now.

The Father created your new beginning from the beginning. Long before you ever knew you'd need one. But you have to walk into it by faith. You have to trust that you've been looking at things from the wrong perspective. It's not over, it's a new start.

For *I know the plans I have for you*," declares the LORD, "plans to prosper you and not to harm you, plans to give you hope and a future.

I believe we spend far too much time thinking about the crucifixion and not nearly enough focus on the resurrection. Our minds naturally want to linger there.

Jesus rose with all the power of heaven and earth. The crucifixion was the path, not the destination. Your troubles are on the path but they are not your destination.

Your destination is a victory. To rise from every adversity through the power of Jesus Christ that lives in you.

"These things I have *spoken unto you, that in me ye might* have *peace. In the* world *ye shall* have *tribulation: but be of good cheer;* I have overcome.*" (John 16:33)*

Your peace is not found in reflecting on the flogging and torture but rather the salvation that resulted from it.

Focus on (1) The salvation of the thief on the cross (2) The compassion He showed his enemies when He said, "Father forgive them for they know not what they do." (Luke 23:34) and (3) victory over death- "Where, O death, is your victory? Where, O death, is your sting?" (1 Cor. 15:55)

His death wasn't the ending. It was just the beginning of your victory. Because of what Jesus did, you will overcome- everything – every time. But you have to see things the way God sees them. Not as problems but as possibilities. Not as endings but as new beginnings.

Don't be afraid to begin anew. There is no shame in starting over. There is no shame in having to begin again. If you are facing a new beginning, embrace it with expectation for greater blessings.

"Remember not the former things, nor consider the things of old. Behold, I am doing a new thing; now it springs forth, do you not perceive it? I will make a way in the wilderness and rivers in the desert." (Isaiah 43:18-19)

~

Whatever you're going through, It could always be much worse, Don't make a mistake, Mistaking your blessing for a curse. –Unknown

~

~

The unthankful heart discovers no mercies;
But the thankful heart will find, In every hour, some heavenly blessings. -Unknown

~

CHAPTER -14

HE (GOD) USES WHOMEVER HE
CHOOSES.

Careful not to judge or condemn. Today's
persecutor may become tomorrow's prophet.
All it takes is a Damascus road experience.
Saul, in the bible, murdered Christians. Even
though at birth God ordained Him for His
kingdom work.

"He who had set me apart before I was born,
and who called me by his grace, was pleased
to reveal his Son to me so that I might
preach him among the Gentiles." (Galatians
1:15-16)

Saul later would be called Paul. God
changed his heart and his purpose. After his
conversion, Paul referred to himself in
Timothy as "chief among sinners".

God has always had a plan for your life. Regardless of where you've ended up, you can always turnaround. The love of Christ wills your heart's desires. No matter what you did in your past that does not cancel out your future.

"This is a faithful saying, and worthy of all acceptation, that Christ Jesus came into the world to save sinners; of whom I am chief." (1Tim 1:15)

God chooses whom He will use. It's not our decision to make. Nor is it our business to judge. If you are in a position where you feel God is calling you to salvation and ministry don't be afraid to pursue God's will.

Find a trusted man or woman of God to mentor you. Sit under their leadership and allow God to speak into your life. You don't need their approval, you just need accountability and support.

I used to feel like God couldn't use me because I'd had a rough start in life. I made poor decisions. I wasn't a model Christian by any means. But God had a different plan.

Everything that I experienced in my past has become a testimony. And to my surprise, when I share them, people are blessed. Sure some people still hold things against me. There will always be those people who make it their business to throw stones. But God sees me differently.

In His eyes, I'm not my mistakes. I am the righteousness of God in Christ. Read Philippians 3:9 for encouragement, "and be found in him, not having a righteousness of my own that comes from the law, but that which is through faith in Christ--the righteousness that comes from God based on faith."

Paul was always painfully aware of what he'd done, hence the chief sinner reference. While there's no denying Paul's murderous past, not one believer would ever dare discount Apostle Paul's work for the Kingdom.

Apart from Jesus, Paul is arguably the most important figure in the New Testament. You may have been a chief sinner in your past, but when God chooses to use you, there will be no denying your God-ordained purpose in the Kingdom.

~
Every obstacle, setback, and
challenges
 In your life is always a blessing in
disguise.
The blessing in disguise is what made
you
Who you are today. Acknowledge
your blessings
And keep moving forward. -Unknown
~

Chapter 15

HIS WAYS ARE NOT OUR WAYS.

The perspective we need is not that of our neighbors, friends, co-workers or best friends. If we want to navigate life without going crazy or stressing out, we have to learn to see every situation through the eyes of God.

Don't meltdown, kneel. "Rejoice always, pray without ceasing, give thanks in all circumstances; for this is the will of God in Christ Jesus for you." (1Thesselonians 5:16-18). In the eyes of God, what's happening is never as bad as it seems. It's working in your favor, but timing is everything. What seems like a disaster today will be a triumph tomorrow.

He's always making a way. Expect favor. "Surely, LORD, you bless the righteous; you surround them with your favor as with a shield." (Psalm 5:12)

He can use anybody. His love transcends mistakes, mishaps, and questionable pasts. None of the people in the Old Testament or new were perfect.

You don't have to be either. Repent for your past. Turn from it. Receive the love of God and accept His forgiveness.

"For my thoughts are not your thoughts, neither are your ways my ways," declares the LORD. "As the heavens are higher than the earth, so are my ways higher than your ways and my thoughts than your thoughts." (Isaiah 55:8-9)

If you don't take away anything else, let Isaiah 55:8-9 become your mantra. God does not think the way we think. He does not handle situations the way we think they should be handled.

In the middle of your circumstance ask yourself, *am I looking at this through God's eyes?*

God sees the whole picture-beginning, middle, and end. Our view is limited to what happened in the past and what we see right this moment. Our trust and faith must be in God.

END

Thank you for reading. I pray that you were encouraged by the words here.

If you feel this is an inspirational message that someone else could benefit from, please leave a comment on Amazon.com for those who may be browsing and considering this book. If you enjoy my latest title, you may also enjoy:

Read the next title(s):

The Struggle Is Real But God's Grace Is Life-Changing
Bible Study Stories and Prayer Devotionals

Renewing Your Mind
A Mindset Book for Spiritual Warfare

Get A Free Audiobook Gift Code While Supplies Last When You Register Your Email Address on my site at IMotivateMyself.com.

Find Out When Books Are Free. Join My Email List.

Made in United States
Orlando, FL
25 May 2022

18181726R00046